# The Focus Fortress

## How to Focus and Find Peace in a Distracted World

Thomas Swain

# Start Your Week The Right Way

We've all had that sinking feeling on a Sunday night, when you remember it's Monday tomorrow and the weekend is over. It can be tricky trying to launch ourselves back into work-mode, but with the right motivation and mentality, you can get your week off to the perfect start.

Receive evidence-based guidance, up-to-date resources, and first-hand accounts to help you.

Sign Up Now & You will receive this newsletter every Monday.

https://www.subscribepage.com/tswain

### You can find me at

instagram.com/swindali

# TABLE OF CONTENTS

Introduction .................................................................................. 1

## PART 1: THE ATTENTION CRISIS ........................................ 9
Chapter 1: Why You Can't Focus ........................................... 10
Chapter 2: The Evolution of Distraction ............................. 26
Chapter 3: Attention is the New Currency ........................ 36
Chapter 4: The Silent Thief ...................................................... 49

## PART 2: REWIRING YOUR FOCUS ................................... 58
Chapter 5: Build Your Focus Fortress ................................. 59
Chapter 6: The Dopamine Detox ........................................... 76
Chapter 7: The Power of Deep Work .................................... 86

## PART 3: LIVING A FOCUSED LIFE .................................... 97
Chapter 8: The Focus Compass .............................................. 98
Chapter 9: Aligning Focus with Values ............................. 116
Conclusion .................................................................................. 126
BONUS: Habit Tracker ............................................................. 134
BONUS: Day Plan & Journal .................................................. 135
REFERENCES ............................................................................. 144

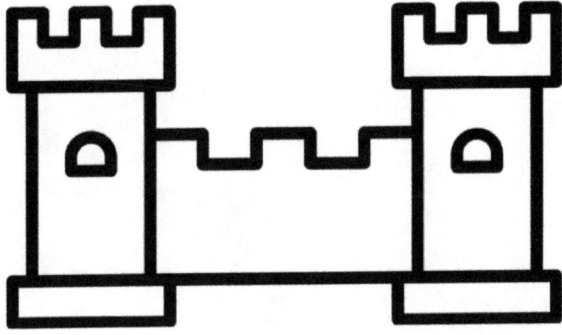

# Introduction

Why does the average person spend more than seven years of their life staring at screens and endlessly scrolling?

*Seven years...*

That's not just a minor distraction; it's a significant drain on our potential. Imagine what you could accomplish in that time. You could master a skill, build a meaningful career, strengthen relationships, or pursue a lifelong dream. Instead, our most valuable resource—our attention—is continually being hijacked by distractions.

But here's the reality: It doesn't have to be this way.

## The Modern Attention Crisis

Today's world is connected like never before and is full of distractions designed to grab your attention. Every app, notification, and platform aims to keep you engaged. This constant stimulation can change how your brain works. It makes it harder to concentrate, think deeply, and connect with what matters most.

The result? A growing attention crisis that steals your time, drains your mental energy, and leaves you feeling disconnected and unfulfilled.

*Distractions don't just waste hours—they steal your life.*

# THE FOCUS FORTRESS

When your attention is scattered, your goals slip further out of reach. Progress stalls, ambitions fade, and days blur into a dull routine of chasing brief pleasures. You're left wondering, "Where did the time go?"

"Why do my dreams remain just dreams?"

But here's the good news: Focus isn't just for a select few people. It's a skill that anyone can learn and get better at with practice. Like training a muscle, you can improve your focus, avoid distractions, and direct your energy toward what matters most.

This book is your roadmap. It's not just about regaining productivity; it's about reclaiming your life.

## The Focus Fortress: A Historical Lesson

In the late 1400s, the island of Rhodes had one of the strongest fortresses in history. The Knights of St. John defended this fortress against powerful opponents, including the Ottoman Empire.

The fortress wasn't strong because of its walls alone. The Knights were alert to their environment. They reinforced their defenses, dug deeper moats, and adjusted to new threats. Their hard work paid off when Sultan Mehmed II, the ruler of the

# THE FOCUS FORTRESS

Ottoman Empire and fresh from conquering Constantinople, attacked Rhodes with a large army.

The lesson is clear: A fortress built strategically, with care and vigilance, can withstand even the toughest attacks.

**Your attention is like that fortress.**

In a world filled with distractions, you need strong defenses to protect your focus and keep you moving toward your goals. Without those defenses, your mind becomes vulnerable to the constant bombardment of notifications, social media, and endless to-do lists.

Building your "Focus Fortress" doesn't happen by accident. It requires intention, strategy, and consistent effort. But once you've fortified your focus, you'll be able to channel your energy toward meaningful tasks, protect your mental clarity, and achieve the goals that matter most.

## Focus is Freedom

Focus gives you freedom. It frees you from distractions. It frees you from feeling overwhelmed. It allows you to live a life based on what matters most to you.

When you reduce distractions and concentrate on meaningful tasks and relationships, you find more peace, fulfillment, and purpose.

Think about the last time you focused on something important.

Remember how good it felt to make real progress. Now, imagine if you could experience that kind of clarity and intention every day.

*Focus is not just about getting more done. It's about enjoying life to the fullest.*

## A Focused Mind is a Happy Mind

A distracted mind is chaotic, restless, and anxious. It's constantly jumping between tasks, bombarded by notifications, and struggling to keep up. This causes mental chaos which creates stress and leaves little room for joy or fulfillment.

A focused mind is calm, clear, and deeply engaged. When you work on a meaningful task and enter a state of flow, your mind quiets. Worries, regrets, and distractions fade away.

This state of flow is one of the most satisfying mental experiences you can have. It's in these moments that you feel truly present, purposeful, and alive.

*Human beings crave purpose.*

We want to feel like we're growing, contributing, and moving forward in life. A focused mind allows you to channel your energy into tasks that align with your values, giving you that sense of progress and fulfillment.

*A focused mind isn't just more productive—it's a happier mind.*

**What You'll Gain from This Book**

This book will give you the tools to reclaim your time, energy, and peace of mind. By the end, you'll experience the power of:

- Beginning each day with clarity
- Progressing through your tasks with purpose
- Concluding the day with a sense of fulfillment

We'll take a three-part journey to transform your relationship with attention and focus:

### The Attention Crisis

We'll explore the roots of modern distractions, uncover the science behind overstimulation, and reveal how technology exploits your brain's natural wiring.

## Rewiring Your Focus

Here's where the transformation happens. You'll learn practical, science-based strategies to reset your brain, strengthen your focus, and build habits that shield your mental clarity.

## Living a Focused Life

Finally, we'll align your newfound focus with your deepest goals. You'll learn how to channel your attention into what matters most, creating a life filled with purpose and momentum.

This guide is not just another collection of generic productivity tips. It provides a clear, step-by-step plan to help you focus, eliminate distractions, and live with purpose.

**Your Journey Begins Now**

Are you ready to take back control of your attention? To build habits and systems that protect your focus and help you achieve your goals?

It's time to break free from the noise, rebuild your mental fortress, and create a life of clarity, purpose, and achievement.

Your journey to a focused life starts now.

# PART 1:
# THE ATTENTION CRISIS

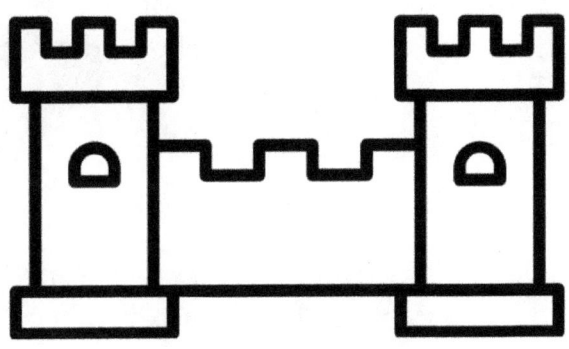

# Chapter 1:
# Why You Can't Focus

Why is it easier to scroll for hours than to sit still for just five minutes?

You sit down to focus on something important, but within moments, a notification appears. Suddenly, half an hour has flown by. By the end of the day, you feel that you've been busy, but you've accomplished nothing meaningful.

Why does this keep happening?

The modern attention crisis isn't simply about willpower or discipline. It's about how technology is changing the way our brains work.

Recent studies show that many people struggle to stay focused. More than half of Americans say they are addicted to their phones, and the numbers are even more striking when we look deeper. On average, people are checking their phones 144 times a day. That's once every ten minutes during their waking hours! Many say they have their phones

# THE FOCUS FORTRESS

with them at all times. They sleep with their phones (60%), check them within the first ten minutes of waking up (89%), and use them on the toilet (75%).

*These aren't just statistics: they're warning signs of a society losing its ability to concentrate.*

However, the most concerning issue is how this behavior affects our younger generations. Studies show that teenagers who spend more than three hours a day on social media are significantly more likely to report mental health problems. The average attention span has reportedly dropped from 12 seconds in 2000 to just 8 seconds today—*shorter than that of a goldfish.*

While these numbers might seem alarming, they're just symptoms of a deeper problem.

## The Attention Economy: Why We're All Targets

We often feel like we can't put our phones down, and there's a good reason for that.

Modern technology is designed to grab our attention.

Social media, streaming services, and mobile apps use smart psychological tricks that make them very engaging and even addictive.

Companies hire teams of psychologists and behavior experts to help create products that keep us coming back for more.

These platforms use several key strategies to capture and hold our attention:

- Variable reward schedules, similar to those used in slot machines, keep us checking our phones repeatedly for new content or likes.
- Infinite scrolling removes natural stopping points, making it harder to disengage.
- Push notifications create a sense of urgency and fear of missing out (FOMO).

## THE FOCUS FORTRESS

- Personalized content algorithms learn our preferences and serve increasingly engaging content.
- Social validation features (likes, comments, shares) tap into our fundamental need for acceptance.
- Gamification elements create artificial goals and rewards.
- Auto-play features remove decision points and encourage continued consumption.
- Strategic use of colors and sounds triggers emotional responses.
- Personalized recommendations create a sense of being understood.
- Social proof indicators normalize excessive usage.

Every day, we face many choices, notifications, and demands. When you sit down to work, your attention gets pulled in many directions. Tasks that should take 20 minutes can end up taking hours. By the end of the day, you may feel tired and unfulfilled. This doesn't concern just our productivity: our ability to think deeply and live with purpose is also affected.

## The Neuroscience of Distraction

But what's really happening inside your brain during these moments of distraction?

For us to understand, we'll need a short neuroscience lesson in which we'll focus on one key player: dopamine.

## Dopamine and the Science of Overstimulation

Dopamine is far more complex than the simple "pleasure chemical" it's often described as. It's an essential neurotransmitter that acts as the brain's text message service, delivering important updates between cells that facilitate communication.

While it does play a crucial role in pleasure and reward, its true function is much broader, influencing everything from motivation and planning to learning and attention.

Dopamine is important for our thinking and emotions. When the dopamine system works well, it helps us focus on important tasks and plan and complete complex activities. It also allows us to feel a real sense of satisfaction when we achieve something

Dopamine drives us to pursue meaningful goals and helps us learn and remember things. It also regulates our emotions. Furthermore, it aids in decision-making, improves our ability to adapt to new situations, and supports our motivation. All of these functions are necessary for pursuing our goals.

However, like many powerful systems in our brain, the dopamine system has a darker side when it's hijacked by modern technology.

**The Dopamine Loop: Why We Can't Stop Scrolling**

Pleasurable experiences, such as food, sex, achievements, or social media notifications, trigger the release of dopamine in our brain's reward system. This system evolved to help our ancestors seek food, shelter, and social connections.

However, modern technology exploits this ancient mechanism in unintended ways.

The dopamine cycle in the digital age typically follows this pattern:

1. **Trigger:** A notification sounds, or you feel a moment of boredom.
2. **Anticipation:** Your brain releases dopamine in anticipation of checking your phone.
3. **Action:** You check the notification or start scrolling.
4. **Reward:** You receive variable rewards (likes, comments, interesting content).
5. **Recovery:** Dopamine levels drop, often below baseline.
6. **Craving:** You feel an urge to repeat the cycle.
7. **Reinforcement:** Each successful cycle strengthens the behavior.
8. **Habituation:** The brain requires more stimulation for the same effect.
9. **Dependency:** The behavior becomes automatic and harder to resist.
10. **Withdrawal:** The absence of stimulation leads to discomfort and anxiety.

# THE FOCUS FORTRESS

This cycle becomes particularly dangerous because digital content is:

- ☑ Always available
- ☑ Never ending
- ☑ Constantly evolving
- ☑ Socially reinforcing
- ☑ Personally tailored
- ☑ Algorithmically optimized
- ☑ Emotionally engaging
- ☑ Accessible with little effort
- ☑ Designed for addiction
- ☑ Culturally normalized

Unlike natural rewards, which are typically limited and require some work to obtain, digital stimulation is available 24/7 with minimal effort. This constant availability leads to what neuroscientists call "dopamine downregulation," where the brain becomes less sensitive to dopamine over time, requiring more stimulation to feel the same level of satisfaction.

# THE FOCUS FORTRESS

**Cognitive Overload**

Imagine your typical day. You wake up and immediately check your phone, responding to messages and scrolling through social media before you're even fully awake. Throughout your morning routine, you listen to podcasts or news updates. At work, you juggle multiple tabs and windows, switching between email, instant messages, and actual work tasks.

During lunch, you catch up on social media while watching YouTube videos. The afternoon brings more task-switching, more notifications, more digital demands. By evening, you're mentally exhausted, but still find yourself mindlessly scrolling through content while "relaxing" in front of Netflix.

This constant digital engagement takes a significant toll on our mental health through:

1. Anxiety and Stress
    - Constant connectivity creates a state of hypervigilance.
    - FOMO generates social anxiety.
    - Information overload triggers stress responses.
    - Comparison with others' curated lives affects self-esteem.
    - The pressure to be always available creates tension.

2. Depression and Mood Disorders
    - Reduced face-to-face interactions affect emotional well-being.
    - Digital addiction can lead to feelings of emptiness.
    - Constant comparison promotes a negative self-image.
    - Reduced physical activity impacts mood regulation.
    - Sleep disruption affects emotional stability.

3. Altered Cognitive Function
    - Attention span deterioration
    - Memory processing issues
    - Reduced creative thinking
    - Impaired decision-making
    - Decreased emotional intelligence

The constant barrage of information and stimulation leads to what researchers call cognitive overload, and its effects are far more serious than just feeling scattered or unproductive.

**The Science of Mental Bandwidth**

Your brain's prefrontal cortex helps you focus, make decisions, and control impulses, but it has limited processing power. Think of it like a computer's RAM: it can only handle so many processes at once before performance starts to suffer.

When you're constantly switching between tasks, apps, and notifications, you're forcing your brain to repeatedly:

1. Interrupt its current processes
2. Save its current state
3. Clear its working memory

## THE FOCUS FORTRESS

4. Load new context
5. Resume processing
6. Monitor for new interruptions
7. Evaluate priorities
8. Manage emotional responses
9. Filter relevant information
10. Maintain goal awareness

This constant context-switching doesn't just slow you down: it fundamentally alters how your brain functions. Research shows that heavy multitaskers struggle with filtering out irrelevant information, managing working memory, and switching between tasks efficiently. They find it harder to maintain sustained attention, resist distractions, and process complex information. This cognitive overload impacts their ability to make strategic decisions, regulate emotions, learn new skills, and form long-term memories.

The statistics on interruptions are startling. According to research from the University of California, Irvine:

- It takes an average of 23 minutes to fully regain focus after an interruption.
- Workers are interrupted every 11 minutes on average.

## THE FOCUS FORTRESS

- People spend only about three minutes on a single task before switching.
- Forty-four percent of interruptions are self-initiated.
- Each interruption increases the likelihood of errors.
- Task completion time can double with frequent interruptions.
- Stress levels rise significantly with each interruption.
- Quality of work decreases with increased interruptions.
- Decision-making ability deteriorates throughout the day.
- Creative thinking is particularly vulnerable to interruptions.

Do the math: if you're interrupted every 11 minutes and it takes 23 minutes to regain focus, you're operating at a constant attention deficit. This helps explain why many people feel busy all day but accomplish little of substance.

THE FOCUS FORTRESS

## The Modern Attention Crisis: By the Numbers

The scope of our collective attention problem becomes clear when we look at the data:

- **Screen Time:** The average adult spends over ten hours per day consuming digital media.
- **Social Media:** Users spend an average of 2 hours and 27 minutes per day on social platforms.
- **Smartphone Usage:** People touch their phones 2,617 times per day on average.

## THE FOCUS FORTRESS

- **Email:** The average worker receives 121 emails per day.
- **Video Content:** People watch over 16 hours of online video per week.

These statistics make it clear that our attention crisis is more than a personal productivity issue. It's a public health challenge with serious implications for society.

However, understanding the problem is the first step toward a solution. Struggles with focus aren't a personal failure or lack of willpower, but a predictable response to an environment designed to capture and monetize attention.

*The path forward begins with recognizing that your brain isn't broken: it's reacting normally to abnormal levels of stimulation.*

**Focus is a skill that can be rebuilt through practice and environmental changes.**

Small adjustments in how you interact with technology can significantly improve your attention, and recovery is possible with consistent effort and awareness.

Building new habits takes time, but creates lasting change. Support systems and accountability accelerate progress, while understanding your triggers can help you avoid reactive behaviors. Mindfulness practices strengthen your ability to focus, and thoughtful environmental design promotes better behavior.

*Remember, progress isn't linear.*

Setbacks are normal, but with persistence, you can regain control of your attention and mental clarity.

The solution doesn't involve digital abstinence or returning to a pre-internet age. Rather, it concerns learning to use technology intentionally.

In the following chapters, we'll explore practical strategies for regaining control of your attention and rebuilding your capacity for deep focus.

But remember: *awareness is the first step.*

Simply understanding how your brain responds to digital stimulation can help you make better choices about how you spend your attention—your most valuable resource in the modern world.

# Chapter 2: The Evolution of Distraction

Distraction has always been a challenge for people, but it changes with our culture and technology. Today, distractions are more common and appealing than ever.

We face notifications, social media updates, and a constant stream of content competing for our attention, all of which make it hard to focus.

Throughout history, famous thinkers like Socrates and Seneca have warned us

about the dangers of wasting time. They knew that a distracted mind can prevent us from living with purpose and fulfillment.

Seneca expressed an important idea that is still relevant today:

*"It is not that we have a short time to live, but that we waste much of it."*

His words remind us that our lives have great potential, but many of us let small distractions take away our important moments.

## Distraction in Ancient Times: A Necessary Escape

In ancient times, people saw distractions as helpful rather than negative. They provided a needed break from the difficulties of life. Ancient Romans went to gladiator games, and Greek philosophers had discussions in marketplaces. Festivals and gatherings gave people a chance to step away from their daily routines.

But these distractions had natural limits. The games ended. The debates ceased. And people returned to their daily lives with clarity. These temporary diversions didn't consume their attention the way modern distractions do.

Today, those natural breaks are gone. Technology provides a never-ending stream of entertainment, news, and social validation. Instead of a brief escape, we live in a constant state of distraction, where our attention is continually pulled in different directions.

**The Turning Point: The Industrial Revolution**

The evolution of distraction took a significant turn during the Industrial Revolution. For the first time, mass production made information and entertainment widely available. Newspapers, magazines, and books were printed in large quantities.

Suddenly, people had more to read, learn, and consume than ever before.

The introduction of radio in the early 20th century took things even further. Families gathered around their radios to hear the latest news, listen to music, or follow radio dramas. But radio broadcasts had fixed schedules, creating natural breaks in the day.

Then came television. In the 1950s, television sets became household staples, revolutionizing how people consumed entertainment. Families no longer gathered to share stories or read books—they sat in front of screens, passively absorbing content. TV shows were captivating, but like radio, they still had defined start and end times.

## The Rise of Personalized Distraction

The evolution of distraction accelerated exponentially with the advent of the internet and smartphones. Unlike radio or TV, the internet never shuts off. Smartphones made distraction portable, giving people instant access to endless content.

Social media platforms like Facebook, Instagram, and Twitter revolutionized the way we interact with information. No longer passive consumers, we became active participants in the attention economy. The more we engaged with content, the more these platforms learned about us, tailoring our feeds to show us exactly what we wanted to see.

This personalization was a game-changer. Instead of broadcasting the same message to everyone, platforms began delivering highly curated content that targeted individual users. The goal? To keep us engaged for as long as possible.

# THE FOCUS FORTRESS

## From Radio to TikTok: How Distractions Have Evolved

Distractions have evolved dramatically over the past century. Here's a quick timeline to illustrate how technology has reshaped our attention spans:

| Era | Main Distractions | Impact on Focus |
|---|---|---|
| 1900s | Newspapers, radio | Scheduled distractions with natural breaks |
| 1950s | Television | Visual entertainment created passive consumption |
| 1980s | Video games, 24-hour news | Interactive distractions; continuous news cycle |
| 2000s | Social media, smartphones | Portable distractions; constant connection |
| 2010s–Present | TikTok, streaming, algorithms | Infinite scrolling; personalized, addictive content |

# THE FOCUS FORTRESS

Each technological advance brought new ways to consume information—and each has chipped away at our ability to focus.

## The Attention Economy: How Distraction Became a Business

In the digital age, attention isn't just a human resource—it's a currency.

The concept of the attention economy explains how tech companies profit from keeping you distracted.

Here's how it works:

- **Tech Companies Create Addictive Experiences:** Platforms like TikTok, YouTube, and Instagram are designed to capture your attention and keep you scrolling. They use endless scrolling, autoplay videos, and notifications to hook you.

- **Advertisers Pay for Your Attention:** The more time you spend on a platform, the more ads you see. Advertisers pay tech companies for access to your attention, turning your time into their revenue.

- **You Become the Product:** Social media isn't free. You're paying with your time, your attention, and your personal data. Platforms track your behavior to deliver more targeted ads and keep you coming back for more.

## Why Modern Distractions Are More Dangerous Than Ever

Unlike past distractions, modern distractions are always available, always personalized, and always escalating. Here's what makes today's distractions so dangerous:

- **Infinite Content:** There's no stopping point. TikTok videos, Instagram Reels, and YouTube playlists are endless. You no longer have to make a conscious decision to continue consuming—they've removed that barrier.

- **Personalized Feeds:** Algorithms curate content specifically for you. The more you engage, the more the platform learns about your preferences, delivering content that's harder to resist.

- **Emotional Manipulation:** Social media taps into basic human emotions like fear, anger, and joy to keep you engaged. Outrageous headlines, shocking videos, and heartwarming stories are strategically placed to trigger emotional responses.

**The Psychology of Modern Distraction**

Distractions today aren't just more frequent—they're more addictive.

Why? Because they play on basic human psychology. Let's break down a few key principles that social media and tech companies use to keep you hooked:

1. **Variable Rewards (The Slot Machine Effect)**
    - Social media operates like a slot machine.

- You don't know what the next post will be—maybe it's funny, maybe it's shocking, maybe it's boring.
- That unpredictability keeps you scrolling, hoping for the next hit.

2. **FOMO**
   - Notifications create a sense of urgency.
   - What if someone messaged you? What if there's breaking news?
   - This fear keeps you checking your phone, even when there's nothing important.

3. **Social Validation**
   - Likes, comments, and shares trigger the brain's reward system.
   - Every notification is a small hit of dopamine, reinforcing the desire to keep posting and engaging.

### Distraction Isn't Going Anywhere

The distractions we face today aren't random—they're carefully designed.

Tech platforms and social media companies do more than just grab your attention by chance: they

## THE FOCUS FORTRESS

create their systems to take advantage of how your brain reacts to new things and rewards.

Each like, notification, and new piece of content is carefully crafted to keep you engaged. What starts as a quick check of your phone can quickly spiral into hours of scrolling through endless feeds. The result?

*Time lost, mental energy drained, and a growing sense of dissatisfaction.*

Distractions take away your time and make it harder to concentrate and think clearly.

This affects your ability to focus on what is important. The results are serious—not just in terms of wasted hours, but also lost opportunities.

If we don't take control of our attention, we risk becoming passive consumers in an economy that profits from our distraction.

The question is: Are you willing to let your life be dictated by algorithms?

Or will you reclaim your focus and take control?

# Chapter 3: Attention is the New Currency

As we covered earlier, since the year 2000, the average human attention span has dropped from twelve seconds to just eight seconds? To put this in perspective, a goldfish has a nine-second attention span.

This isn't just an interesting fact: it's a cautionary message.

Today, your attention is a commodity. Tech companies are in a constant race to capture it—and they're making billions in the process.

This concept is known as *the attention economy*, where *time spent equals revenue*. The more time you spend on a platform, the more ads you see, and the more data they gather to sell to advertisers. It's a simple formula that fuels a multi-billion-dollar industry.

# THE FOCUS FORTRESS

## How Social Media Algorithms Hijack Your Attention

If radio and TV broadcasters essentially threw their messages into the air at random, modern social media is more like a laser-guided missile aimed directly at your brain.

Platforms like Facebook, Instagram, TikTok, and YouTube aren't just sharing information but are actively competing for your attention. Why? Because attention is money. The more time you spend with them, the more ads they can show you, and the more data about you they can collect.

## THE FOCUS FORTRESS

But they don't just wait for you to log in. They lure you in with carefully crafted algorithms that:

- ☑ **Track Your Behavior:** Every like, click, and scroll tells the algorithm what you're interested in.

- ☑ **Personalize Your Feed:** Your feed is curated to show you content that will keep you engaged.

- ☑ **Trigger Emotional Responses:** The algorithm shows you content that evokes strong emotions—such as laughter, outrage, or sadness—to keep you hooked.

Social media algorithms are designed to create dopamine loops—endless cycles of seeking and receiving small rewards that keep you scrolling. Every notification, every like, every new piece of content gives you a dopamine hit, reinforcing the behavior.

Put simply, social media platforms create addictive experiences to keep you engaged, advertisers pay for access to your attention, and your time and data are sold, which makes you the product.

*Attention is the currency of the digital age.* But, unlike money, once you spend your attention, the time it consumes is gone forever.

# THE FOCUS FORTRESS

Consider this:

- The average person spends **2.5 hours a day on social media.**
- That's *17.5 hours a week*, or *38 days a year.*
- Over a lifetime, that adds up to more than *7 years spent scrolling.*

Imagine what you could achieve with that time if you directed it toward meaningful goals instead.

In the 21st century, your attention isn't just a habit; it's become a form of currency. Right now, your attention is being stolen. Like money, attention can be stolen, wasted, or wisely invested. The problem

## THE FOCUS FORTRESS

is that most of us don't even realize when it's slipping through our fingers.

Every notification you receive, every ad that catches your attention, every autoplay video, every scroll is designed to hijack your focus. The addictive nature of notifications, endless scrolling, and autoplay is engineered to trap you.

Ever opened your phone to check one email and ended up spending 30 minutes on Instagram? You pick up your phone to check one quick notification. Maybe it's a text or a headline. Before you know it, 20 minutes have disappeared into a blur of TikTok videos, Instagram Reels, or Facebook updates. Each swipe feels satisfying at the moment, thanks to the small dopamine hits that come with novelty.

But when you finally put your phone down, there's an empty feeling. What did you actually accomplish? Probably nothing meaningful. Instead of focusing on a project or goal, or even intentionally relaxing, your mind has been hijacked by an endless cycle of passive consumption.

This isn't a coincidence. Tech platforms are designed to make it hard to stop. Infinite scroll features and autoplay videos are engineered to keep you hooked, feeding your brain a steady stream of dopamine hits.

Here are a few ways this happens in the modern world:

**Autoplay: One More Episode Syndrome**

Streaming services like Netflix and YouTube are experts at stealing your attention. You finish one episode of a show, and before you can decide to get up or move on, the next one is already playing. What was supposed to be a single episode turns into three hours of binge-watching a show you might not even care about.

These small, seemingly harmless choices add up. What could have been an evening spent working on a side project, enjoying a hobby, or spending quality time with family is lost in a fog of mindless consumption.

**Notifications**

Notifications are like small, constant interruptions. A single ping from your phone, whether it's a text, a like on a social media post, or an email, pulls you out of the moment. Maybe you're working on an important task, having a conversation, or even enjoying some quiet time. However, that notification demands your immediate attention and breaks your focus.

## THE FOCUS FORTRESS

Over time, this constant state of interruption conditions your brain to expect and seek out distractions, even when none are present. You may find yourself obsessively checking your phone , even when there aren't any notifications, just in case you missed something! It's not just your time that's being wasted: it's also your ability to concentrate deeply that's at risk.

### Porn

Today, porn is one of our biggest attention traps. It hijacks your brain's reward system, delivering instant dopamine hits that make it difficult to pull away. What begins as a "quick visit" can turn into hours of consumption, leaving you feeling drained, guilty, and disconnected from real-world intimacy.

And the issue involves more than explicit porn. Soft porn—the kind you encounter on social media—is everywhere. Thirst traps, provocative dance videos, or images of "perfect" bodies trigger the same dopamine response as explicit porn. It's all designed to exploit your biological urges, making it nearly impossible to stop scrolling.

Over time, this constant exposure rewires your brain, making it harder for you to find fulfillment in meaningful relationships and activities. Instead of building real connections or focusing on your

## THE FOCUS FORTRESS

personal growth, you get caught in a loop of chasing fleeting pleasures that ultimately leave you feeling unhappy.

### Drama

Have you ever found yourself arguing about, or getting angry at, something completely trivial? Whether it's politics, a celebrity scandal, a contentious review, a news item, or some other kind of drama, it draws you in, consuming hours of your time and leaving you emotionally drained. But drama in any form rarely leads to meaningful outcomes. Instead, it pulls your focus away from what truly matters: your goals, relationships, and personal growth. Ultimately, you're left with feelings of regret and frustration.

### Mindless Binge-Watching or Browsing

How many times have you sat down to relax, only to realize you've wasted an entire evening aimlessly flipping through shows or browsing online stores for things you don't need? This type of distraction feels harmless at the moment, but it's a thief of opportunity.

Every moment spent in mindless consumption is a moment that could have been spent pursuing a passion, exercising, reading, or connecting with others. These lost hours accumulate into weeks, months, and even years of unrealized potential.

## Chatting Aimlessly

We all need social interaction, but there's a fine line between meaningful conversation and endless, aimless chatting. Messaging apps, group chats, and DMs make it easy to fall into long, superficial exchanges that go nowhere.

You might start with a quick "Hey, what's up?" and suddenly find yourself deep in a two-hour conversation about nothing significant. Or you get drawn into a group chat filled with memes, gossip, and random updates that add no real value to your life.

These conversations give the illusion of connection, but they often leave you feeling more drained than fulfilled. Instead of investing your time in deep, meaningful relationships or personal growth, you've spent hours talking about absolutely nothing of substance.

The solution? Be intentional with your conversations. Prioritize quality over quantity. Ask yourself: Is this interaction adding value, or am I just killing time?

# THE FOCUS FORTRESS

## The Real Issue: The Hidden Cost of Wasted Attention

The real danger of these distractions isn't just the time they steal, but the opportunities they distract you from. Modern companies compete for your attention to generate profit. The price you pay isn't necessarily money. It's something worth much, much more. You're paying with your life's most valuable resource: *your attention.*

These days, your attention is the most valuable currency available. Companies like social media platforms, streaming services, and advertisers have turned it into a commodity, engineering their systems to extract as much of it as possible. This is

## THE FOCUS FORTRESS

the foundation of the attention economy: a marketplace where your focus is bought and sold.

The longer you stay engaged, the more ads you see, and the more data they collect about your behavior. Every second you spend scrolling or watching generates revenue for these platforms. Features like infinite scroll, autoplay, and push notifications aren't accidental. They're deliberate tools designed to keep you hooked.

The goal isn't just to capture your attention temporarily but to condition you to return repeatedly, creating a habit.

Imagine your attention as a gold mine. Social media, news outlets, and streaming platforms send their metaphorical miners (notifications, algorithms, and autoplay features) into your mental gold mine to extract as much as possible. They leave you depleted, while they profit from your time and focus.

Think about it like this: Imagine if your bank account was slowly drained every time you scrolled social media or got lost in a binge-watching session. That would make you panic, wouldn't it? Yet, we allow our attention to be taken away from us every day without even realizing what it's costing us.

# THE FOCUS FORTRESS

Just like the cash in your wallet, your attention is finite. There's only so much you have available to spend each day. But unlike money, you can't earn back the time spent on wasted attention. It's gone forever.

We often become our own worst enemies. We waste attention on things that don't matter. Pointless arguments, mindless scrolling, or binge-watching shows we don't even like. The real issue is that every moment wasted could have been used to build your dreams, deepen relationships, or improve yourself.

## Your Attention is Finite

Once spent, it's gone forever. Unlike money, you can't earn more hours in the day or recharge your mental capacity once it's depleted. Think of your attention like fuel in a tank. Every notification, message, or moment spent scrolling uses up a bit of that precious energy. By the time you want to focus on something meaningful. Your goals, your relationships, or your personal growth, you're running on empty.

You could also think of your attention as a daily budget. Each morning, you wake up with a finite amount of "mental dollars" to spend. Every task, notification, or distraction deducts from this

## THE FOCUS FORTRESS

balance. Checking your phone first thing in the morning? That's $10 gone. Answering personal emails during work hours when you're deeply involved in a task? Another $20. Endless scrolling before bed? There goes the rest of your account.

At the end of the day, most of us realize we've spent our entire budget on things that don't matter, leaving nothing for the goals, people, or activities that truly enrich our lives. Unlike money, this budget resets daily, but the opportunities you missed—finishing a project, connecting with loved ones, or simply resting—are lost forever.

Understanding that your attention is a limited, non-renewable resource is the first step. Recognizing the mechanisms of the attention economy is the second. When you realize how valuable your focus is and how much effort is spent trying to take it from you, you can begin to take back control.

Ask yourself: Where is my attention going? Is it building the life I want, or is it being siphoned off for someone else's profit? Protect your attention like the precious resource it is, because once it's gone, so are the opportunities it could have created.

# Chapter 4: The Silent Thief

Imagine leaving your front door slightly ajar each day....

At first, you barely notice. It seems harmless. But over time, someone begins slipping inside, taking small things. A book here, a few coins there. It may not alarm you at first. But months later, you look around and realize your home feels empty.

Things are missing, and you have no idea where they've all gone.

This is what distractions do to us. They don't steal our attention all at once. They sneak in gradually, moment by moment, until we're left wondering how hours, days, and even years have slipped through our fingers.

Distractions take away more than just brief moments: they deprive you of your presence with your loved ones and your ability to focus on what truly matters.

They can even diminish your sense of control over your own life. Over time, distractions increase stress, speed up the aging process, and leave you questioning where the years have gone.

A distracted life isn't just a busy one. It's a life not fully lived.

**Getting punched in the face**

I'll never forget the day I realized how costly distractions can be.

It was a tough lesson that showed me the importance of staying focused. I practice Muay Thai, and during a sparring session, I faced a fighter from a professional fight club. A group of professional fighters watched us closely as we started. My opponent was very intense. Sparring is

## THE FOCUS FORTRESS

usually more relaxed, but this guy was going full power with every punch.

Midway through the round, my mind started to wander. Instead of focusing on my timing, skills, and technique—the things I could control—I began to worry about how I looked, whether the pro fighters were impressed, and if they thought I belonged there.

In that brief moment of distraction, my opponent landed a clear shot to my face. I stumbled back, struggling to understand what had just happened, and then another blow hit me.

I fell hard to the mat.

When I stood up, I was dazed and had two black eyes and a cut with blood running down my face. I had been given a harsh reminder of my lack of focus..

In combat sports, a moment of distraction can decide whether you stay standing or get knocked down. The lesson is clear: if you don't focus on what you're doing, you'll face the consequences.

This idea applies outside the ring as well.

Distractions, no matter how small, can sneak up on you, sabotage your progress, and knock you off course, whether that's worrying about what others think or letting your mind drift to things you can't control.

The outcome is the same: you lose.

## Distraction Is Not Harmless

Distraction is a silent thief that infiltrates every corner of our lives, stealing not only time but also the connections, health, and goals that make life meaningful. Let's break down the personal toll that distractions take.

### Mental Health

Chronic overstimulation is linked to higher rates of anxiety, depression, and social isolation. Many people struggle to sit alone with their thoughts without reaching for a digital escape. When you're constantly pulled in multiple directions—juggling notifications, work, and endless scrolling—your brain remains in a heightened state of activity, increasing your stress level.

### Chronic distractions can lead to:

- **Burnout**: The constant task-switching exhausts your mental reserves, leaving you unable to fully recharge.

- **Sleep Disruption**: Late-night screen time and overstimulation make it harder for you to unwind, leading to poor-quality rest.
- **Increased Anxiety:** The pressure for you to respond to every notification or keep up with endless feeds contributes to feelings of overwhelm and inadequacy.

## Physical health

Even physical health isn't spared by the costs of distractions. Sedentary habits like prolonged screen time are linked to issues like weight gain, back pain, and weakened cardiovascular health. Over time, these seemingly small behaviors compound, harming both your body and mind.

## Future prospects

Distractions not only affect your current focus but can also interfere with your future success. Every moment spent on mindless activities is a moment stolen from pursuing meaningful goals. Whether it's building a career, writing a book, or learning a new skill, distractions keep you stuck in a loop of instant gratification, preventing long-term progress.

Instead of moving toward your dreams, you find yourself procrastinating, stuck in analysis paralysis, or too drained to make meaningful progress. The result? Days, months, even years slip away with little to show for your efforts.

Worse, distractions can erode the discipline and habits you need for success.

Goals require sustained effort and focus, but a distracted mind struggles to maintain momentum, leaving you frustrated and falling short of your potential

## Relationships

Distractions prevent us from being completely present with our loved ones. Instead of fully engaging in conversations, we divide our attention between screens and people, leading to emotional disconnection.

When distractions overwhelm your attention, they pull you away from the people who matter most. Think about how often your conversations are interrupted by phone notifications or how moments of shared silence are filled with you scrolling through social media. These seemingly small choices chip away at the quality of your connections.

Over time, this constant fragmentation of attention leaves loved ones feeling undervalued and unheard. Eye contact is replaced by glances at a screen, and deep conversations give way to shallow exchanges. Relationships flourish with genuine presence, while distractions create emotional distance even when physically close.

**Distraction Data**

Research confirms the dangerous impact distractions have on our lives:

## Health

A study published in the journal *JAMA Network Open* found that individuals who engage in heavy screen time and multitasking are more likely to experience poor mental health outcomes, including depression and emotional instability. Constant notifications keep the brain in a hyper-alert state, making it harder to unwind, relax, and focus on long-term well-being.

## Productivity

A study by Microsoft found that after an interruption, employees take an average of 15 minutes to fully re-engage with their original task. Even more concerning, they often engage in non-related tasks before returning to their work, further delaying progress. These micro-distractions compound throughout the day, resulting in significant productivity loss.

## Relationships

A study published in the journal *Computers in Human Behavior* found that the mere presence of a smartphone during a conversation—even if it isn't used—can reduce the quality of connection and trust between people. This phenomenon, called "phubbing" (phone snubbing), illustrates how distractions erode interpersonal bonds.

### The Big Picture

Distractions have far-reaching consequences.

They don't just steal brief moments; they undermine your most important relationships, drain your energy, and restrict you from creating the life you desire.

When distractions aren't dealt with, they can make you feel isolated, unfulfilled, and questioning where the years have gone.

The good news?

These costs are avoidable. By recognizing the problem and taking steps to reclaim your attention, you can rebuild stronger connections, improve your well-being, and move boldly toward your goals.

Once you understand how distractions weaken your relationships, health, and goals, you can begin building the habits and systems to reclaim your attention. It's not about being perfect but rather making progress: small, intentional changes that can transform how you engage with the world.

In the next chapter, we'll explore how to train your mind, build focus like a muscle, and create a framework to protect your attention against the constant pull of modern life.

Your potential hasn't disappeared—it's just waiting for you to take back control.

Let's start rebuilding, one step at a time.

# PART 2:
# REWIRING YOUR FOCUS

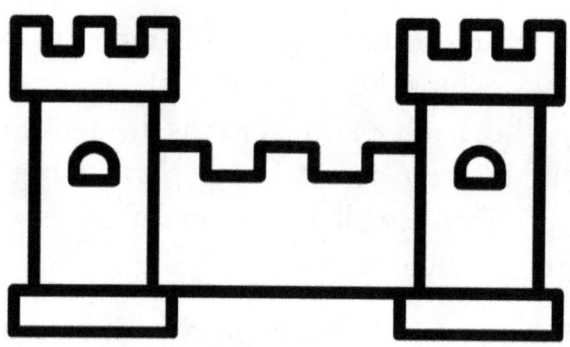

# Chapter 5: Build Your Focus Fortress

In the late 1400s, the island of Rhodes was home to one of the most impenetrable fortresses in history. Defended by the Knights of St. John, the fortress faced multiple attacks by some of the most powerful armies of its time, including the Ottoman Empire.

The walls of Rhodes were not only built with stone; they were strengthened with strategy and vigilance. The defenders constantly strengthened their walls, dug moats, and adjusted their defenses to adapt to new threats.

When the Ottoman forces, led by Sultan Mehmed II, launched a full-scale attack on Rhodes, they expected a quick victory. Despite their overwhelming numbers and advanced weapons, they were unable to breach the walls. The fortress stood strong, showing that effective defenses can endure even the most determined attackers.

# THE FOCUS FORTRESS

## Building Your Focus Fortress

Distractions pull your attention in different directions, making it hard to concentrate. Without protection for your focus, you may feel overwhelmed and unproductive.

The good news is that you can take control.

Think of your focus as a fortress, where you keep your valuable resources: time, energy, and attention. Your defenses should be strong, flexible, and regularly reinforced to guard against distractions. With effort, you can build strong defenses that protect your attention and keep your mind sharp.

## THE FOCUS FORTRESS

In today's world, many distractions constantly attack your focus. Notifications, emails, social media, and wandering thoughts can invade your concentration. Willpower alone won't keep them out. You need effective systems and habits to protect your attention and stay focused on what matters most.

Think back to the famous fortress in Rhodes. If the walls had been weak or the gates left open, enemy forces would have easily taken it. This situation is similar to your focus. Without clear boundaries and intentional practices, distractions can slip in, disrupting your ability to work, think, and live with purpose.

Building a Focus Fortress isn't about achieving a distraction-free life.

That's impossible. Instead, it's about designing an environment and habits that minimize interruptions and support your goals. Each system or habit you put in place is a brick in your fortress wall. Over time, those small actions create unbreakable defenses that protect your attention from distractions and help you achieve meaningful progress.

Just as a well-constructed fortress can withstand even the most determined sieges, your focus systems protect you from the constant barrage of modern distractions. And here's the best part:

Building your Focus Fortress isn't complicated.

## Small Habits, Big Results

Building your Focus Fortress doesn't require dramatic changes.

Instead, you make small, deliberate habits that compound over time. By creating systems to protect your attention, you're not only enhancing your productivity but also preserving your mental clarity, creativity, and peace of mind.

Here's how to start:

### Step 1: Plan and Prioritize Your Day

Without a clear plan, distractions will creep in. Planning your day helps you stay on track and direct your focus toward meaningful tasks.

How to Do It:

- At the start of each day or near the end of the day, list your tasks in order of priority.
- Make the first part of your day focused on deep work tasks that require full

concentration. For example, writing, problem-solving, or creative projects.

- Treat these periods as sacred focus zones where *distractions aren't allowed.*

(You can find a day planner at the end of this book in the bonus section.)

## Step 2: Start Small with Timed Sessions

Just like building physical strength, mental focus takes time to develop. Don't expect to work for hours without distraction right away.

How to Do It:

- Start with short focus sessions. Even five minutes is enough to begin.
- Use a timing system (like the Pomodoro Technique) to work for 25 minutes and take a 5-minute break. Take a walk or stand up. No phone or surfing the net.
- Gradually increase your focus sessions over time.

## Step 3: Track Your Progress

Tracking your focus sessions keeps you accountable and shows you how far you've come.

# THE FOCUS FORTRESS

How to Do It:

- Use a habit tracker or journal to log your focus sessions.
- Record what worked, what distracted you, and how you felt afterward.
- Celebrate small wins to keep yourself motivated.

(You can find a habit tracker at the end of this book in the bonus section.)

## Step 4: Build a Focus Ritual

Rituals signal to your brain that it's time to focus, making it easier to enter a deep work state.

How to Do It:

- Create a pre-work routine by brewing coffee, lighting a candle, or spending five minutes journaling before starting work.
- Stick to the same time of day for focused work to build consistency.

**Reset Your Mind for Deeper Focus**

Imagine building a fortress to protect your attention, only to realize that the noise isn't coming from outside—it's inside the walls. Even the strongest defenses won't help if your mind is overstimulated from within.

Every time you receive a notification, email, or see a headline, your brain releases dopamine, a reward chemical. These small bursts of dopamine can make you feel accomplished when you reply to a message, like a post, or scroll through the news.

However, you're not really making progress. Instead, you're just moving from one distraction to another.

The result?

Mental fatigue, poor concentration, and decision paralysis. Constant stimulation leaves no room for creativity, reflection, or deep work. It's no wonder we feel exhausted and scattered at the end of the day.

So, what's the solution?

To achieve true mental clarity, you need to do more than block external distractions.

You need to reset your brain.

This reset is about clearing the mental clutter from overstimulation. Reducing the noise in your mind helps you think deeper, be more creative, and focus better.

Here's how to do it:

## Step 1: Limit Your Phone Use (Your Biggest Source of Overstimulation)

Your smartphone is the main culprit behind modern-day overstimulation. It's always within reach, tempting you to check it during every pause. If you're serious about reclaiming your focus, you need to set boundaries.

- **Morning Rule: Start Your Day Without Your Phone**
  **Why:** Checking your phone first thing floods your brain with distractions before it's had a chance to wake up.
  **What to Do:** Avoid checking your phone

for at least the first hour after waking up. Use this time for quiet activities like journaling, planning your day, or working on a project.

- **Night Rule: Unplug Before Bed**
  **Why:** Screen time before bed interferes with your sleep, keeping your brain alert when it should be winding down.
  **What to Do:** Turn off your phone at least an hour before bed. Replace screen time with calming activities like reading or meditating to unwind naturally.

- **Daily Cap: Limit Non-Essential Screen Time**
  **Why:** The average person spends over three hours a day on their phone. That's time that could be used more meaningfully.
  **What to Do:** Set a daily limit of one to two hours of non-essential phone use. Use apps like ScreenTime (iPhone) or Digital Wellbeing (Android) to track your usage and stay accountable.

## Step 2: Create Tech-Free Zones

Creating tech-free zones in your home or workspace can significantly reduce mental clutter and improve focus. They act as physical reminders to stay present and reduce distractions.

Here's how to set them up:

- **The Bedroom:** Keep your phone out of the bedroom to improve sleep quality and create a calmer space for rest.
- **The Dining Table:** Use meals as a chance, without screens, to connect with loved ones or reflect on your day.
- **Work Blocks:** Dedicate specific hours to deep work without open email, social media, or messaging apps.

## Step 3: Embrace Boredom (A Secret Weapon for Clarity)

In a world that treats boredom like a disease, we've trained ourselves to avoid it at all costs. But boredom isn't your enemy, but actually the birthplace of your best ideas.

When your brain isn't constantly consuming new information, it has the space to connect ideas, solve problems, and spark creativity. Here's why boredom matters:

- **Your Brain Needs Space to Think**: Creativity doesn't come from constant input: it comes from processing. If you're always consuming—whether it's social media, news, or entertainment—your brain has no time to connect ideas or generate original thoughts.

- **Overloaded Minds Can't Focus**: Every distraction drains your mental energy. Over time, this makes it harder to concentrate on deep work.

- **The Fear of Stillness**: Many of us feel uncomfortable being alone with our thoughts. But it's in these quiet moments that clarity emerges.

The irony is clear: the more we try to escape boredom, the more we lose the creativity and focus we're searching for.

### Step 4: Practice the "Boredom Challenge"

To reset your brain, you need to retrain yourself to sit with stillness. The Boredom Challenge is a simple way to do this.

Here's how to start:

- **Try a Technology-Free Morning**: Leave your phone in another room for the first hour of your day.

- **Take a Walk Without Your Phone:** Focus on your surroundings, the rhythm of your steps, and your breathing.

- **Mindful Journaling**: Use a notebook to freely write down your thoughts, decluttering your mind and sparking creativity.

## Step 5: Rediscover Quiet Activities

Replace constant screen use with calming, low-stimulation activities that promote clarity.

Here are a few ideas:

- **Mindful Walking**: Take a walk without headphones or a phone. Notice the sights, sounds, and sensations around you.

- **Meditation**: Spend a few minutes in quiet reflection, focusing on your breath or a simple mantra. Apps like Insight Timer or Headspace can help guide beginners.

- **Journaling**: Free-write your thoughts to process emotions and spark ideas.

- **Mindful Eating**: Have a meal without distractions, paying attention to your food's flavors and textures, and the act of eating itself.

## Step 6: Create Rituals of Stillness

Incorporate intentional pauses throughout your day to reset your mental state. These rituals help calm your mind and create space for clarity.

Here's how to do it:

- **Morning Reset**: Start your day with 10 to 15 minutes of silence or light movement instead of checking your phone.

- **Midday Break**: Step away from work for 10 minutes to reflect or engage in light movement.

## THE FOCUS FORTRESS

- **Evening Wind-Down**: Turn off screens at least an hour before bed to let your mind unwind naturally.

**Why Focus Creates a Ripple Effect**

When we allow ourselves to sit with stillness and reduce distractions, we reclaim control over our attention. It's in these quiet moments that we solve problems, connect ideas, and rediscover our direction.

Reducing stimulation isn't about doing less, but about doing what matters.

By resetting your brain and embracing boredom, you'll unlock creativity, focus, and your full potential.

Focus isn't limited to the moment you're in—it encompasses how those moments build upon each other over time.

Many people believe that focus is an innate talent. Something that some people are born with, and others aren't. But this is a myth: focus is a skill. Just like building muscles at the gym, consistent training and intentional practice are required to grow stronger over time.

## THE FOCUS FORTRESS

Imagine going to the gym for one great workout and then never returning. Would you expect to see lasting results? Of course not. The same goes for focus. One productive day won't change your life. But daily, deliberate practice will.

Each time you commit to focused work, you're strengthening your mental resilience. And just like with physical fitness, the more you train your focus, the easier it becomes to sustain deep attention and push distractions aside.

When I first started practicing deliberate focus, I could barely concentrate for five minutes. I'd set a timer, sit down to work, and almost immediately feel the urge to check my phone or switch tasks. Honestly, I was worse than a goldfish.

But I stuck with it. I started with short sessions—five minutes of uninterrupted work, then ten, then twenty. It wasn't easy, but with consistent effort, I slowly strengthened my focus.

A few months in, the change was undeniable. I could sit down to work without distractions, complete tasks faster, and even enjoy the process. Focus wasn't a struggle anymore, it was a skill I had mastered.

Each time you commit your full attention to a task, you're building momentum. Over days, weeks, and months, that momentum compounds into extraordinary results.

This is the secret behind high achievers: They understand that focus creates a ripple effect.

- **Success Compounds**: You achieve more, faster, because your efforts build on each other.

- **Creativity Flows**: With fewer distractions, your mind connects ideas and generates breakthroughs.

- **Fulfillment Grows**: You feel a deep sense of satisfaction knowing your time is aligned with your goals.

## Focus is Freedom

Your Focus Fortress isn't just about productivity. Ultimately it's about regaining control of your time and attention. When you build strong habits and systems, you stop reacting to the endless distractions around you. Instead, you become intentional about your work, your goals, and your life. Focus isn't a talent. It's a skill that compounds over time. Each small step you take today strengthens your mental defenses, helping you create a life of clarity, purpose, and achievement.

Your Focus Fortress is built!

## THE FOCUS FORTRESS

You've established boundaries, systems, and habits to guard your most valuable resource: your attention. But you aren't supposed to stay behind the walls. Your fortress is meant to be the stronghold from which you launch your most meaningful pursuits.

In addition to protecting your time from distractions, focus involves living with intention and directing your attention toward the goals and values that matter most.

This brings us to the next step: living a focused life.

What's the point of protecting your attention if it's not aimed at the things that truly move the needle? Your fortress walls give you the space to think, reflect, and focus deeply. Now, it's time to use that clarity to take action.

In the following chapters, we'll explore how to align your attention with your goals. Because focus without direction is just another form of distraction.

But before that, there is one last thing to introduce to you.

# Chapter 6: The Dopamine Detox

Imagine being able to reset your brain and regain focus that distractions have taken away. A dopamine detox can help you escape the cycle of overstimulation. It allows you to calm your mind and find clarity.

The concept is simple. Our modern world is overloaded with instant gratification. From social media notifications to streaming platforms, everything is designed to capture and hold your attention by triggering small, addictive dopamine hits. Over time, this constant stimulation rewires your brain to crave more, leaving you feeling restless, distracted, and dissatisfied.

*A dopamine detox is about breaking that cycle.*

It's not about eliminating dopamine—it's essential for motivation and pleasure. Rather, you will reduce your dependence on dopamine and learn to appreciate the deeper, slower rewards that come from focus, creativity, and meaningful connection.

# THE FOCUS FORTRESS

## Why We Need a Dopamine Detox

In the past, moments of stillness and boredom were unavoidable. People spent time in quiet reflection, and entertainment had natural breaks. But today, distractions are constant and limitless. There's always another video to watch, notification to check, or feed to scroll. The result?

Cognitive exhaustion and emotional burnout.

Your brain seeks new experiences because they release dopamine, which makes you feel good. This helped our ancestors explore and survive. Today, however, this natural response is often misused.

Notifications, likes, and autoplay videos give quick dopamine boosts, leading you to want more. Over time, this changes how your brain works, making it harder to focus on tasks that don't provide instant rewards. Activities requiring deep focus—like reading, solving problems, or having meaningful conversations—can start to feel uninteresting.

The problem isn't dopamine itself. The problem is overstimulation.

Just like a muscle can't work endlessly without rest, your brain needs breaks from the constant bombardment of novelty. Without these breaks, your mind becomes fatigued, making it harder to think clearly, solve problems, or feel satisfaction.

**What Happens to Your Brain During a Detox?**

When you reduce your exposure to high-stimulation activities, your brain goes through a withdrawal period. At first, you'll feel restless, bored, and even anxious. This discomfort is a sign that your brain is adjusting to the lack of constant dopamine hits.

But after this initial discomfort, something powerful happens.

Your brain begins to rewire itself. It starts finding pleasure in slower, more meaningful activities.

## THE FOCUS FORTRESS

You'll notice that tasks you once avoided, like reading, journaling, or simply sitting in silence, become more enjoyable. Your ability to concentrate improves. You feel more present. You begin to crave meaningful rewards over instant gratification.

This process is essential for rebuilding your focus. A distracted mind is a restless mind. A focused mind is a calm, fulfilled mind.

## Practical Steps for a Dopamine Detox

### Identify Your Triggers

The first step in a dopamine detox is identifying what overstimulates you. For most people, it's their phone. Social media, notifications, binge-watching, and mindless scrolling are common culprits. But it can also be excessive news consumption, video games, or even constant background noise.

### Start with Small Changes

You don't need to go completely tech-free to see results. Start by setting boundaries around your most overstimulating habits. For example:

- Avoid checking your phone first thing in the morning.

- Create "no-phone zones" in your home, like the bedroom or dining table.
- Limit screen time before bed to improve sleep quality.

**Embrace Boredom**

Modern society teaches us that boredom is bad. But boredom is a powerful tool for clarity and creativity. When you let your mind wander without distractions, it starts making connections, solving problems, and generating ideas.

Instead of filling every idle moment with your phone, let yourself be bored. Go for a walk without headphones. Sit quietly for 10 minutes. Let your brain rest from the constant need for novelty.

**Replace High-Stimulation Activities with Low-Stimulation Ones**

Instead of scrolling endlessly through social media, replace that time with calming activities:

- **Reading:** Choose a physical book to avoid the temptation of notifications.
- **Mindful journaling:** Write down your thoughts, ideas, or reflections.

THE FOCUS FORTRESS

- **Walking:** Go outside without your phone. Notice your surroundings, the rhythm of your steps, and your breathing.
- **Creative hobbies:** Painting, writing, or playing an instrument are great ways to engage your mind without overstimulating it.

## Schedule "Digital Detox" Days

Choose one day a week to unplug from all high-stimulation activities. Spend this time on low-stimulation tasks like cooking, spending time with loved ones, or being in nature. Use this time to reset your mind and recharge your mental energy.

### The Benefits of a Dopamine Detox

The results of a dopamine detox are tangible. Here's what you can expect:

### Improved Focus

Without constant distractions, your brain can concentrate on deeper, more meaningful work. Tasks that once felt overwhelming become manageable.

## Increased Productivity

With fewer interruptions, you'll get more done in less time. You'll also find that you can complete tasks with greater accuracy and creativity.

## Greater Emotional Stability

Constant stimulation makes you anxious and restless. A detox calms your mind, reducing anxiety and improving your mood.

## Better Sleep

Reducing screen time before bed improves sleep quality, helping you wake up feeling more refreshed.

## Deeper Fulfillment

When you remove instant gratification, you make room for slower, more meaningful rewards. You'll find joy in activities that align with your values and goals.

## Common Misconceptions About a Dopamine Detox

Let's address a few myths:

*"I have to give up technology forever."*

No you won't. A dopamine detox is about creating healthy boundaries with technology, not eliminating it completely.

*"I'll be bored the entire time."*

Yes, boredom is part of the process. But boredom leads to clarity, creativity, and deep thinking.

*"It won't make a difference."*

Even small changes, like limiting phone use in the morning, can significantly improve your focus and mental clarity.

**A Simple Dopamine Reset Routine**

Here's a simple routine to incorporate a dopamine detox into your life:

1. Morning:
    - Start your day with a tech-free hour.
    - Journal your thoughts.
    - Plan your day.
    - Enjoy your breakfast without screens.
2. Midday:
    - Take a tech-free walk.
    - Leave your phone at home or put it on airplane mode.

- Notice the sights, sounds, and sensations around you.

3. Evening:
    - Unplug at least one hour before bed.
    - Read a book.
    - Practice mindfulness or meditation.
    - Reflect on your day.

## Final Thoughts: The Power of a Mental Reset

A dopamine detox isn't meant to punish you, but to give you a path to freedom from the endless cycle of distractions that hijack your mind and drain your

## THE FOCUS FORTRESS

energy. By reducing overstimulation, you create space for clarity, focus, and meaningful experiences.

*Remember, distractions aren't going away.*

The world will continue to bombard you with notifications, pings, and updates. But by taking control of your dopamine triggers, you take the first step toward reclaiming your mental clarity and living a more intentional life.

The more you reduce overstimulation, the more you reconnect with what truly matters. The question is: Will you take the first step?

# Chapter 7:
# The Power of Deep Work

In today's fast-paced world, distractions like notifications, social media, and digital entertainment make it hard to focus. Many people struggle to keep their attention, often getting stuck in shallow tasks that don't bring satisfaction or real progress. This type of work is very different from deep work, which means dedicating focused time to tackle complex tasks that need concentration and mental effort.

*What sets high achievers apart is their practice of deep work.*

They realize that success doesn't necessarily come from working longer or harder, but from working smarter and with intention.

By creating an environment that encourages focused work, they give their minds the space to dive deep into tasks. This helps them improve their thinking, creativity, problem-solving skills, and overall productivity. Adopting this mindset and building habits that support deep work can lead to significant personal and professional growth, helping people achieve their biggest goals.

**Focused Success in a Distracted World**

Cal Newport, the author of *Deep Work: Rules for Focused Success in a Distracted World*, explains that deep work is the antidote to a distracted life.

It's the ability to focus on what truly matters without interruption—a skill that's becoming increasingly rare in today's attention economy. But for those who can cultivate it, deep work is a game-changer.

## Shallow Work vs. Deep Work: Understanding the Difference

Most people live in a state of shallow work without realizing it. They move from task to task, never diving deep enough to produce something meaningful. Shallow work feels productive, but it rarely leads to breakthroughs or significant progress.

Shallow work is about staying busy. Deep work is about getting results.

Shallow work includes things like responding to emails, attending meetings, scrolling social media, and handling administrative tasks. These activities aren't cognitively demanding and are easily replicated by others.

In contrast, deep work requires sustained concentration on tasks that are difficult to replicate—tasks that create real value and drive long-term success.

Imagine two writers. One spends the day bouncing between emails and social media and drafting paragraphs between interruptions. The other spends two focused hours writing in complete silence, with no distractions.

## THE FOCUS FORTRESS

The first writer may feel busy all day, but they'll likely produce fragmented work. The second writer will achieve far more in two hours of deep work than the first writer accomplishes in an entire day of shallow work.

This principle applies to nearly every field—from scientists and entrepreneurs to artists and programmers. The ability to focus deeply is the competitive edge that separates mediocrity from mastery.

### Why Deep Work Matters

Today, deep work is a superpower, not only because it leads to better results but because it brings something we crave in our distracted lives: fulfillment.

Distractions break our focus and use up our energy, making us feel tired and unproductive. When we concentrate on deep work, we enter a state of flow. In this state, we become fully engaged in a task and lose track of time. This is when creativity thrives, and we solve complex problems and make real progress.

# THE FOCUS FORTRESS

**Deep work leads to:**

- **Higher-Quality Output:** With sustained focus, your work is more thoughtful and refined.
- **Greater Efficiency:** Tasks that might take you hours in a distracted state can be completed in less time when you focus deeply.
- **Increased Fulfillment:** Deep work is inherently satisfying. It feels good to make real progress on something important.

But most people rarely experience this state of focus. Instead, their days are filled with distractions and interruptions. Reclaiming deep work isn't just about productivity—it's about reclaiming your mind.

## The Stories of Deep Work Practitioners

Throughout history, some of the world's most successful individuals have used deep work to achieve their greatest accomplishments. Let's take a closer look at two powerful examples.

### Carl Jung: Building a Fortress for His Mind

Carl Jung, one of the most influential psychiatrists of the 20th century, understood the importance of deep work long before the term existed. In the early 1920s, as Jung's reputation grew, so did the demands on his time. He was overwhelmed with patients, lectures, and correspondence, leaving little room for the deep thinking he needed to develop his theories.

To solve this problem, Jung built a retreat in the Swiss countryside called the Bollingen Tower. He would reside there for weeks at a time, completely disconnected from the outside world, to engage in deep, uninterrupted thought. It was during these periods of solitude that Jung developed some of his most groundbreaking ideas in psychology, including his work on the collective unconscious.

Jung's story teaches us that deep work requires intentional boundaries. He didn't wait for quiet moments to appear—he created them. In a world filled with noise, he built a literal fortress to protect his mind.

## J.K. Rowling: Finishing Harry Potter in Isolation

Even in modern times, deep work remains essential for creative breakthroughs. In 2007, as J.K. Rowling was finishing the final book in the Harry Potter series, she found herself overwhelmed by distractions. She realized that working from home wasn't cutting it—her phone rang constantly, emails piled up, and her family needed her attention.

Desperate to finish the book, Rowling checked into a hotel in Edinburgh. There, she isolated herself from the outside world to focus entirely on writing. In this environment, free from distractions, she completed Harry Potter and the Deathly Hallows, which was one of the most successful books of all time.

Rowling's story highlights a crucial point: deep work requires intentional separation from distractions. It's not sufficient to simply wish to focus: you must take specific steps to establish an environment that fosters deep work.

## How to Carve Out Deep Work Sessions

Deep work doesn't happen by accident. You have to design your environment and routines to support it. Here are some practical strategies to incorporate deep work into your daily life.

### Time-Blocking for Deep Work

Time-blocking is a simple but powerful technique for scheduling deep work. Instead of letting your day unfold reactively, set aside specific blocks of time for focused, uninterrupted work.

How it works:

- Block out at least 90 minutes for deep work sessions. During this time, eliminate all distractions. Turn off notifications, close unnecessary tabs, and let others know you're unavailable.

Why it works:

- Your brain needs time to settle into deep focus. Short bursts of work won't achieve this. A dedicated block of time allows you to enter a state of flow.

THE FOCUS FORTRESS

## Design Your Environment for Focus

Your surroundings play a significant role in your ability to focus. Distractions are everywhere, but you can minimize them with a few intentional changes.

How to do it:

- Create a workspace that signals deep work. This could be a specific room, a desk with no clutter, or even a coffee shop where you feel productive. Remove distractions. off your phone, use noise-canceling headphones, and keep your space minimal.

Why it works:

- When your environment supports focus, it's easier to slip into deep work. Think of it as building your own mental Bollingen Tower.

## Establish a Pre-Work Ritual

Your brain responds to rituals. Creating a pre-work ritual signals to your mind that it's time to focus, making it easier to transition into deep work.

How to do it:

- Develop a simple routine before each deep work session. This could be making a cup of coffee, lighting a candle, or spending five minutes journaling. Over time, your brain will associate this ritual with entering a focused state.

## The Rewards of Deep Work

Deep work isn't just a productivity tool; rather, it's a life-changing practice. It allows you to achieve more in less time, reduce mental clutter, and experience greater fulfillment.

The most successful people in the world don't work more hours—they work better hours. They carve out time for deep work, focusing their energy on the tasks that truly matter.

When you commit to deep work, you'll:

- Create higher-quality work.
- Make faster progress toward your goals.
- Feel more fulfilled and less overwhelmed.
- Unlock your creative potential.

Deep work is your competitive advantage in a world of shallow distractions. It's how you create meaningful work, achieve your goals, and build a life filled with purpose.

## THE FOCUS FORTRESS

Distractions will always be there, pulling at your attention. But deep work is your superpower. It's the key to unlocking your full potential and creating something truly valuable.

The question is: Will you let distractions dictate your life, or will you carve out time for the work that matters most?

# PART 3:
# LIVING A FOCUSED LIFE

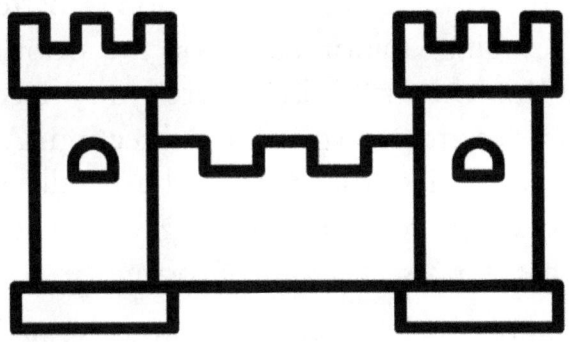

# Chapter 8:
# The Focus Compass

What truly deserves your attention, and are you giving it enough?

In a world full of distractions, it's easy to let your focus drift toward things that don't matter, like doom scrolling, minor tasks, or the priorities of others. But the truth is, where you place your attention determines your life's direction. Are you focusing on what truly moves the needle toward your goals, or are you scattering your energy on things that don't serve your purpose?

To effectively direct your attention, you need a guide that aligns your focus with what truly matters. This is where the Focus Compass comes in. Like a traditional compass, this tool helps you find clarity and direction. It keeps you focused on what matters, avoiding distractions and guiding you toward your goals.

# THE FOCUS FORTRESS

## The Focus Compass

The Focus Compass has four points:

| North: Purpose | South: Energy |
|---|---|
| Your purpose is your "true north." It's what drives you and gives your actions meaning. Without a clear purpose, your focus will scatter, leaving you feeling unfulfilled. Defining your purpose ensures your efforts align with your values and long-term goals. | Just as a compass needs a magnetic field to point true, you need energy to maintain focus. Your physical and mental well-being—supported by adequate sleep, nutrition, and exercise—forms the foundation for sustained attention. Without energy, even the clearest goals can seem impossible. |

## THE FOCUS FORTRESS

| East: Tools | West: Recovery |
|---|---|
| Tools are the practical strategies and systems that keep your focus on track. These include apps, planners, and routines that streamline your day, helping you prioritize what matters and avoid distractions. | Recovery is the often-overlooked key to maintaining focus. Rest, reflection, and moments of stillness allow your mind to recharge, ensuring you're ready to give your best. Without recovery, burnout is inevitable, and focus becomes impossible. |

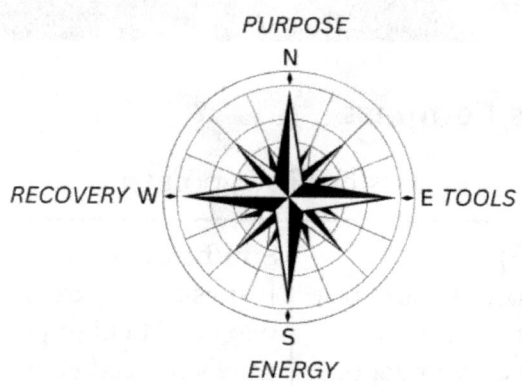

As you can see, the Focus Compass has the following features at each of its cardinal points:

1. **Purpose (North):** Your purpose is your "true north." It's what drives you and gives your actions meaning. Without a clear purpose, your focus will scatter, leaving you

feeling unfulfilled. Defining your purpose ensures your efforts align with your values and long-term goals.
2. **Energy (South):** Just as a compass needs a magnetic field to point true, you need energy to maintain focus. Your physical and mental well-being—supported by adequate sleep, nutrition, and exercise—forms the foundation for sustained attention. Without energy, even the clearest goals can seem impossible.
3. **Tools (East):** Tools are the practical strategies and systems that keep your focus on track. These include apps, planners, and routines that streamline your day, helping you prioritize what matters and avoid distractions.
4. **Recovery (West):** Recovery is the often-overlooked key to maintaining focus. Rest, reflection, and moments of stillness allow your mind to recharge, ensuring you're ready to give your best. Without recovery, burnout is inevitable, and focus becomes impossible.

The Focus Compass is a complete system. Each part supports the others, helping you balance and focus your attention effectively.

## Practical Steps:

By using the Focus Compass framework, you can take actionable steps to ensure your attention aligns with your goals. Here's how to implement each point:

### 1. Define Your Purpose (North)

Your purpose is your guiding star. Without it, your efforts lack direction.

- **Write It Down:** Reflect on what truly matters to you. Ask questions like, "What do I want to achieve in the next year? Five years? What values guide me?"

  _____
  _____
  _____
  _____

- **Set Clear Goals:** Break your purpose into actionable milestones. For example, if your purpose is to improve your health, set goals like losing 10 pounds or running a 5K.

  _____
  _____

# THE FOCUS FORTRESS

- **Revisit Regularly:** Keep your purpose visible. Write it on a sticky note or journal about it weekly to stay connected to your "true north."

## 2. Optimize Your Energy (South)

You can't focus effectively if you're running on empty. Building and maintaining energy is essential.

- **Prioritize Sleep**: Aim for seven to nine hours of quality sleep per night. Stick to consistent sleep and wake times to regulate your body clock.

- **Fuel Your Body**: Choose whole, nutrient-dense foods that provide sustained energy. Stay hydrated throughout the day.

- **Move Your Body**: Incorporate daily exercise, even if it's just a ten-minute walk.

Physical activity boosts cognitive function and focus.

- **Take Breaks**: Use techniques like the Pomodoro Technique to balance focus with short rests, ensuring you avoid mental fatigue.

## 3. Use Focus Tools (East)

Leverage practical systems to keep distractions at bay and maintain clarity.

- **Task Prioritization**: Use tools like the Eisenhower Matrix to categorize tasks by urgency and importance, focusing on high-priority items first.

- **Digital Helpers**: Apps like Trello, Notion, or Todoist can streamline planning and task management.

- **Automate**: Set up automated bill payments, email filters, and recurring task reminders to minimize decision fatigue.

## 4. Prioritize Rest and Recovery (West)

Without recovery, your focus will falter. Make rest a part of your strategy.

- **Unplug**: Schedule tech-free times during your day to recharge.

- **Practice Mindfulness**: Spend a few minutes each day meditating, journaling, or reflecting. This quiet time helps reset your mental clarity.

- **Plan Recovery Days**: Take a full day off weekly to relax, pursue hobbies, and reset mentally and physically.

- **Utilize Sleep Rituals**: Develop an evening wind-down routine—dim the lights, read, or practice deep breathing to signal your body it's time to rest.

Follow these steps to focus on your goals and make sure your time and energy go to what matters most. When your attention is scattered, you may feel like you're not making any progress. But when you focus on your purpose, every effort counts.

The Focus Compass can help you stay aligned, directing your energy toward what is truly important while avoiding distractions that sap your strength.

## THE FOCUS FORTRESS

Start by defining your purpose.

Then, optimize your energy, use the right tools, and prioritize rest. This approach will protect your attention and help you move forward clearly and purposefully. Each day is an opportunity to make progress toward your goals instead of just going in circles.

Focus means working smarter and more intentionally, not harder. When you use the Focus Compass to guide your efforts, you will find that the time and energy you invest are valuable.

They help you build a life of purpose and achievement.

# THE FOCUS FORTRESS

## Putting the Focus Compass into Action

Clarity isn't enough on its own.

Knowing what matters is one thing—consistently acting on it is what brings real transformation. The Focus Compass gives you direction, but progress requires action. You're not aiming for perfection or monumental leaps forward, but daily, intentional steps that align with your purpose

Think of each focused day as a brick in your fortress and a step toward your goals.

The more consistent you are, the stronger your foundation becomes.

But consistency doesn't happen by accident. It requires commitment and a plan.

## Focus Fortified

What if you could reclaim hours of lost time, break free from distractions, and finally make progress on your biggest goals?

This isn't about doing more. It's I'm not saying that you should do more. I'm saying you should do what matters most to you—with clarity, intention, and focus. doing what matters most—with clarity, intention, and focus.

# THE FOCUS FORTRESS

For the next 30 days, you will follow a clear plan that will help you reset your habits, improve your focus, and align your actions with your goals. Each day, you'll take simple, manageable steps that build momentum. Over time, these intentional efforts will lead to great results

This challenge is your opportunity to take back control of your attention and build a life filled with purpose and progress. Are you ready to take control of your life?

## The 30-Day Challenge

Now, this isn't just another productivity challenge. This is your blueprint to reclaim your attention and protect it for the long term.

Over the next month, you'll:

- Eliminate distractions that drain your focus.
- Strengthen your ability to stay on task.
- Align your actions with what matters most.
- Build routines that simplify your life and preserve your mental clarity.

Each day, you'll pick up a small change—like a new habit, a helpful strategy, or a boundary—that helps build your Focus Fortress. These tweaks aren't huge transformations but easy, practical adjustments that can blend into any lifestyle.

By the end of the 30 days, you'll have:

- ☑ More mental clarity.
- ☑ Stronger focus habits.
- ☑ Progress toward your goals.

*... and most importantly, a renewed sense of control over your time and attention.*

This isn't about perfection, it's about progress.

One step at a time.

One habit at a time.

One day at a time.

Ready to begin? Let's start building the life you've been distracted from.

## Week 1: Audit Distractions and Eliminate Leaks

- Purpose: Identify where your focus is being stolen and plug the gaps.
- Steps:

# THE FOCUS FORTRESS

- o Track your distractions for one day. Write down every time you check your phone, switch tasks, or lose focus.
- o Turn off non-essential notifications on your phone and computer.
- o Declutter your workspace, removing items that don't contribute to your productivity.
- o Set boundaries for email and social media use (e.g., check only twice a day).
- o Reflect at the end of the week: What are your biggest distractions?

_____
_____
_____
_____

## Week 2: Start Focus Workouts

- Purpose: Build your focus muscle with deliberate practice.
- Steps:
    - o Start with short, timed focus sessions (e.g., ten minutes of deep work). Use a timer to stay on track.

- Gradually increase your focus time each day or every few days. Work toward 20, 30, or 40 minutes by the end of the week.
- Use tools like the Pomodoro Technique to balance focused work with short breaks.
- Track your progress: How long can you focus without distractions?
- Celebrate small wins, such as completing a challenging task in one session.

_____

_____

_____

_____

## Week 3: Align Focus with Goals Using the Focus Compass

- Purpose: Focus your attention on what matters most.
- Steps:
  - **Define your purpose (North):** Write down your key goals and why they matter to you.

- Optimize your energy (South): Commit to getting seven to nine hours of sleep, eating well, and exercising regularly.
- Use tools (East): Plan your tasks each day with a checklist or planner. Prioritize the most important ones.
- Prioritize recovery (West): Schedule moments of rest, reflection, or mindfulness daily.
- Review at the end of the week: Are your actions aligning with your purpose? Adjust as needed.

_____
_____
_____
_____

## Week 4: Refine Routines and Sustain Habits

- Purpose: Cement your focus systems into daily life.
- Steps:

## THE FOCUS FORTRESS

- Review what worked over the past three weeks. Identify habits that felt natural and effective.
- Eliminate or adjust any habits that felt forced or unhelpful.
- Create a "Focus Blueprint"—a simple daily routine that incorporates your best habits from the challenge.
- Share your progress with a friend or mentor for accountability.
- Plan your next 30 days with focus in mind, setting new goals to continue building momentum.

_____
_____
_____
_____

Starting a new habit or breaking old patterns can feel overwhelming, but remember this: *progress is made through small, consistent steps.*

You don't need to overhaul your life in one day. Each little action you take, whether it's tracking distractions, completing a focused workout, or reflecting on your goals, builds momentum.

## THE FOCUS FORTRESS

It's okay to stumble or feel frustrated along the way. What matters most is showing up each day, even if all you can manage is five minutes of focus. Every effort counts, and over time, those small wins will add up to something extraordinary.

You're not in this alone.

Many people have felt the pull of distractions and struggled to reclaim their attention. The key is to trust the process, stay consistent, and celebrate your progress as it comes.

*Attention is your most valuable resource.*

Don't let distractions steal it any longer. The next 30 days are your opportunity to take control, build powerful habits, and create a life of clarity and purpose.

**Start today.**

Commit to this challenge and take the first step toward transforming your focus. Whether it's turning off notifications, setting a timer for your first focus workout, or reflecting on your goals, each small action brings you closer to the results you've been striving for.

Your journey starts now. Are you ready to build your mental fortress, achieve your goals, and

## THE FOCUS FORTRESS

reclaim your life? You can do this. All you have to do is take it one focused moment at a time.

*"Great things are not done by impulse, but by a series of small things brought together."*

—Vincent van Gogh

# Chapter 9: Aligning Focus with Values

We all want to be productive. We set goals, make to-do lists, and track our progress. Yet, even when we tick off every box, many of us are left feeling restless or unsatisfied.

Why?

*Because productivity without purpose feels hollow.*

Working hard can lead to success, but if your actions don't reflect your core values, that success may not bring you fulfillment. You might feel busy but not truly accomplished. You may meet deadlines yet still sense something is lacking. Over time, the disconnect between your efforts and your values can lower your motivation and sap your energy.

The solution? *Align your focus with your values.*

When your daily actions match what is important to you, your life has meaning. You feel that your time is used well, your work is meaningful, and your focus helps you build a life that reflects who you are.

**Why Alignment Matters**

Imagine climbing a mountain, sweating and straining to reach the summit. But when you get there, you realize it's the wrong mountain.

You've been climbing the wrong peak all along.

This is what happens when your focus doesn't match your values. Many people spend years chasing achievements that don't really matter to them. We often follow what society expects, pursue goals set by others, or seek temporary pleasures without stopping to ask if these goals align with what we truly want.

Think about how often you've felt busy but disconnected:

- Working late on a project you don't care about.
- Spending time with people who drain your energy.
- Scrolling through your phone for hours, only to feel empty afterward.

When your focus is misaligned, life becomes a series of meaningless tasks. You feel exhausted, yet strangely unfulfilled.

But when you align your focus with your values, every action gains significance. You're no longer climbing random mountains. You're on the path that leads to your personal summit—the life you truly want to live.

## Living in Alignment: The Power of Clarity

When Carl Jung built his stone tower in Bollingen, Switzerland, he was not just creating a retreat. He was making a clear symbol of his values.

# THE FOCUS FORTRESS

Jung believed that self-reflection, solitude, and creativity are powerful tools. He saw the importance of stepping away from modern distractions to reconnect with deeper truths. His tower became a sanctuary where he could focus on what mattered most: his inner work.

Jung decided to align his life with his core values. He did this not to chase success or recognition, but to live authentically. His goal was to create an environment that supported his most meaningful work.

The lesson? When you align your focus with your values, you find clarity. Your decisions become easier. Your time feels well spent. And you experience a deeper sense of fulfillment.

But how do you know what your core values are? And how can you ensure your daily habits reflect them?

## What Are Core Values?

Your core values are the guiding principles that define who you are and what you stand for. They shape your decisions, your priorities, and your sense of purpose.

## THE FOCUS FORTRESS

For example:

- If freedom is a core value, you might prioritize flexibility in your work and lifestyle.
- If connection is a core value, you'll invest time in building meaningful relationships.
- If growth is a core value, you'll seek opportunities to learn, improve, and challenge yourself.

When you uphold your core values, life feels aligned. Your actions resonate with your beliefs. However, when you disregard your values, life feels chaotic and unfulfilling.

# THE FOCUS FORTRESS

The problem is, many people never take the time to define their values. Instead, they live by default, reacting to external demands and societal pressures, without asking themselves what they truly care about.

## Identifying Your Core Values

Take a moment to reflect on your life.

Think about the times when you've felt most fulfilled, proud, or energized.

What values were you honoring in those moments?

For example:

- Was it authenticity? Did you speak your truth in a difficult situation?
- Was it creativity? Did you complete a passion project that sparked joy?
- Was it connection? Did you spend quality time with loved ones?

Now, think about the moments when you felt drained, frustrated, or disconnected.

What values were you neglecting?

For example:

- Were you compromising your health by overworking and neglecting rest?
- Were you sacrificing your freedom by saying yes to obligations you didn't want?
- Were you ignoring your need for growth by staying in a stagnant job?

These moments reveal your core values—the principles that, when honored, bring meaning to your life.

## The Danger of Misalignment

J.K. Rowling famously wrote the first Harry Potter book while struggling as a single mother. She had very little time, money, or support. But despite the odds, she stayed focused on her writing because it aligned with her core values of creativity and storytelling.

Rowling wasn't driven by fame or fortune. She wrote because it was what mattered most to her. Her focus wasn't scattered on trivial tasks or societal expectations. She directed her limited energy toward what she valued most—and it paid off.

But imagine if Rowling had prioritized tasks that didn't align with her values. Imagine if she spent her time chasing social validation or worrying about her finances instead of writing. We might never have heard of Harry Potter.

This is the danger of misaligned focus: you miss out on your greatest opportunities.

When you spend your attention on things that don't matter to you, you rob yourself of the chance to make meaningful progress on the things that do.

## Aligning Focus with Your Daily Habits

Once you've identified your core values, the next step is to ensure your daily habits reflect them.

For example:

- If health is a core value, are you prioritizing exercise, rest, and nutrition in your daily routine?
- If connection is a core value, are you investing time in building meaningful relationships?
- If creativity is a core value, are you carving out time for passion projects?

# THE FOCUS FORTRESS

It's not enough to set long-term goals that reflect your values. You need to integrate those values into your daily life.

The key is to ask yourself before making decisions, *"Does this action align with my values?"*

For instance:

- Before saying yes to a meeting, ask yourself: Is this worth my time?
- Before starting a new project, ask yourself: Does this align with my long-term vision?
- Before spending hours scrolling through your phone, ask yourself: Is this how I want to spend my time?

When your daily actions align with your values, life feels meaningful. You're not just busy—you're making progress on what matters most.

## The Ripple Effect of Alignment

When your focus aligns with your values, everything changes.

- ☑ You feel more motivated.
- ☑ You experience less stress.
- ☑ You make better decisions.

## THE FOCUS FORTRESS

☑ You find greater fulfillment.

This alignment creates a ripple effect in your life:

- Your work becomes more meaningful.
- Your relationships become deeper and more rewarding.
- Your mental clarity improves.

Think of it as building a life that reflects who you truly are, not who society expects you to be.

At the end of your life, what will matter most?

- It won't be how many tasks you checked off your to-do list.
- It won't be how much money you made.
- It won't be how many followers you had on social media.

What will matter is whether you lived in alignment with your values.

*… and whether you spent your time on what truly mattered to you.*

When you align your focus with your values, you're not just working toward goals. You're building a life of purpose, fulfillment, and meaning.

*And that's the true power of focus.*

# Conclusion

We live in a world where *your attention is under siege.* Every notification, every social media post, and every endless scroll is a calculated attempt to pull you away from what truly matters. This isn't just a minor annoyance. It's an epidemic that's stealing your time, draining your energy, and leaving you feeling scattered and unfulfilled.

But here's the reality: *distraction doesn't have to own you.*

In this book, we have revealed how modern technology takes advantage of your brain's natural wiring to keep you engaged. We've explored how overstimulation diminishes your ability to concentrate, and how a distracted mind can lead to missed opportunities. We also explored the hidden costs of this crisis. Not only in terms of productivity but also in your creativity, relationships, and sense of purpose. But the power to reclaim your focus is already within you.

Focus isn't some rare gift reserved for monks or geniuses.

## THE FOCUS FORTRESS

It's a skill you can cultivate.

In the same way you train your body through exercise, you can strengthen your mind through deliberate practice. Every time you resist a distraction, you're reinforcing your ability to concentrate. Every time you prioritize deep work, you're rewiring your brain to stay present and engaged.

Think of this journey as building your mental fortress.

Each strategy you've learned is a brick in the wall. A defense against the endless stream of noise trying to pull you away from what truly matters.

But a fortress is only as strong as the vigilance of its defenders.

In today's world, distractions are relentless. New apps, new platforms, and new forms of digital seduction will continue to emerge. The challenge isn't to eliminate distractions completely—it's to *control your response* to them. It's to ensure that your time and energy are invested intentionally, in ways that align with your goals and values.

# THE FOCUS FORTRESS

## Your Focus Is Your Freedom

When you reclaim your focus, you're not just improving your productivity—you're taking back your life. Imagine waking up each day with clarity and purpose, knowing exactly where to direct your time and energy. Picture a life where you're no longer at the mercy of notifications, distractions, or endless scrolling. Instead, your work flows smoothly. Your relationships deepen. Your goals, once distant dreams, become attainable milestones that you actively pursue.

*This is the life that focus unlocks.*

# THE FOCUS FORTRESS

It's a life where you have the mental space to think deeply, create meaningfully, and connect wholeheartedly. It's a life where *you're in control of your attention*, not tech companies, not advertisers, not algorithms.

The path to this life isn't complicated, but it does require commitment. It's about taking *small, consistent steps every day*. Silencing notifications, setting boundaries, and embracing moments of stillness. All of these actions compound over time, reshaping your habits and reclaiming your mental clarity.

## The Power of Small, Intentional Actions

Many of us believe that reclaiming focus requires a complete overhaul of their lives. But the truth is, *lasting change happens through small, intentional actions.*

- It starts with turning off notifications for just one hour.
- It starts with dedicating 20 minutes to deep work without interruptions.
- It starts with choosing to be fully present in conversations instead of reaching for your phone.

These actions may seem insignificant at first but they build momentum. And that momentum leads to transformation.

Consider this:

If you improve your focus by just 1% each day, by the end of a year, your ability to concentrate will have improved exponentially. The compounding effect of small changes is what drives lasting success.

Focus isn't a switch you flip overnight. It's a *muscle you strengthen over time.* Every small win reinforces your mental resilience, making it easier to stay on track, even when distractions try to pull you off course.

# THE FOCUS FORTRESS

## Aligning Focus with What Truly Matters

Reclaiming your focus is about more than getting things done. It's about making sure that *what you're focusing on aligns with your values and long-term goals.*

In a world full of noise, it's easy to get swept up in other people's priorities. But a focused life is an intentional life. One where your attention is directed toward the things that bring you joy, fulfillment, and progress.

Ask yourself:

- What are the things in your life that truly matter?
- How much of your daily attention is spent on those things?
- Where can you redirect your focus to better align with your values and aspirations?

## Embracing the Journey

Reclaiming your focus isn't about perfection. There will be days when distractions win. There will be moments when you fall back into old habits.

What matters is *showing up again and again.*

The process of building your mental fortress is ongoing. Every day is a new opportunity to strengthen your defenses, refine your habits, and align your actions with your goals.

Remember: Your mind isn't broken—it's just overwhelmed.

With the tools you've gained in this book, you now have the power to quiet the noise, strengthen your focus, and create a life of clarity, creativity, and purpose.

## Your Focus Defines Your Future

Your attention is the foundation of everything you build in life. It shapes your decisions, your relationships, and your achievements. The things you focus on today will determine the life you wake up to tomorrow.

Protect your attention fiercely.

Invest it wisely.

And watch as it unlocks opportunities you never thought possible.

The power to reclaim your focus is already within you.

*All that's left is to begin.*

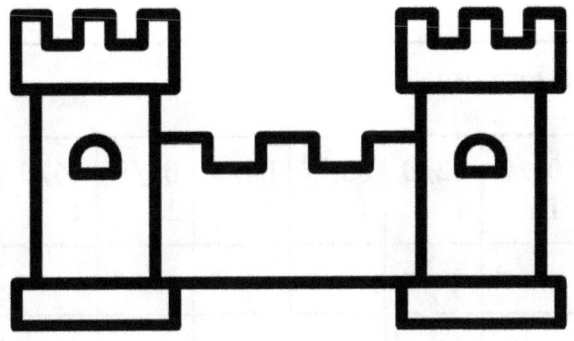

# BONUS: Habit Tracker

Enter the habits you want to track each month. Then check them each day you complete them.

| Month: January | | | | | | | |
|---|---|---|---|---|---|---|---|
| Habit | 01/01 | 02/01 | 03/01 | 04/01 | 05/01 | 06/01 | 07/01 |
| 1 | • | • | • | • | • | • | • |
| 2 | • | • | • | • | • | • | • |
| 3 | • | • | • | • | • | • | • |
| 4 | • | • | • | • | • | • | • |
| 5 | • | • | • | • | • | • | • |
| 6 | • | • | • | • | • | • | • |
| 7 | • | • | • | • | • | • | • |

# BONUS: Day Plan & Journal

Duplicate this every day and fill in the details.

DAY PLAN: [Add the date here]

Learning: [Add what you plan to learn here]

Main Tasks: [Add your three main tasks here]

Timeline: [Work in 30-min blocks. Fill them in.]

8:00 AM - 8:30 AM:
8:30 AM - 9:00 AM:
9:00 AM - 9:30 AM:
9:30 AM - 10:00 AM:

10:00 AM - 10:30 AM:

10:30 AM - 11:00 AM:
11:00 AM - 11:30 AM:
11:30 AM - 12:00 PM:

12:00 PM - 12:30 PM:
12:30 PM - 1:00 PM:
1:00 PM - 1:30 PM:
1:30 PM - 2:00 PM:

2:00 PM - 2:30 PM:
2:30 PM - 3:00 PM:

# THE FOCUS FORTRESS

3:00 PM - 3:30 PM:
3:30 PM - 4:00 PM:

4:00 PM - 4:30 PM:
4:30 PM - 5:00 PM:
5:00 PM - 5:30 PM:
5:30 PM - 6:00 PM:

6:00 PM - 6:30 PM:
6:30 PM - 7:00 PM:
7:00 PM - 7:30 PM:
7:30 PM - 8:00 PM:

8:00 PM - 8:30 PM:
8:30 PM - 9:00 PM:
9:00 PM - 9:30 PM:
9:30 PM - 10:00 PM:

10:00 PM - 10:30 PM:
10:30 PM - 11:00 PM:
11:00 PM - 12:00 AM:

End of the day [Add the date here]

- How was my day?
- What did I achieve?
- What went well?
- What can I improve?
- How was my productivity?
- Essentially in a nutshell what did I do?

## Start Your Week The Right Way

We've all had that sinking feeling on a Sunday night, when you remember it's Monday tomorrow and the weekend is over. It can be tricky trying to launch ourselves back into work-mode, but with the right motivation and mentality, you can get your week off to the perfect start.

Receive evidence-based guidance, up-to-date resources, and first-hand accounts to help you.

Sign Up Now & You will receive this newsletter every Monday.

https://www.subscribepage.com/tswain

You can find me at

instagram.com/swindali

## Discover More Books by Thomas Swain

I hope you enjoyed reading this book! I would greatly appreciate any feedback you have—kindly share it at the place of purchase.

Here are some of my other books:

**Branding: The Fast & Easy Way To Create a Successful Brand That Connects, Sells & Stands Out From The Crowd**

https://www.amazon.com/dp/B09BF1K8G7

THE FOCUS FORTRESS

Mental Toughness & Mindset: Life Lessons From Stoicism & Ancient Spartan Philosophy + A Guide on How to Stop Overthinking (3 books in 1)

https://www.amazon.com/dp/B09YS52J56

THE FOCUS FORTRESS

**Overthinking: How to Stop Overthinking, Escape Negative Thoughts, Declutter Your Mind, Relieve Stress & Anxiety, Build Mental Toughness & Live Fully: Thinking Positively, Self-Esteem, Success Habits**

https://www.amazon.com/dp/B096Z8CFJZ

# THE FOCUS FORTRESS

**Way of The Spartan: Life Lessons To Strengthen Your Character, Build Mental Toughness, Mindset, Self Discipline & A Healthy Body**

https://www.amazon.com/dp/B09FKK32M1

Way of The Stoic: Life Lessons From Stoicism to Strengthen Your Character, Build Mental Toughness, Emotional Resilience, Mindset, Self Discipline & Wisdom

https://www.amazon.com/dp/B09WNFM2SJ

# THE FOCUS FORTRESS

El Camino Del Estoico: Lecciones de vida del estoicismo para fortalecer tu carácter, desarrollar la fortaleza mental (Spanish Edition)
https://www.amazon.com/dp/B0CXPHX466

You can find me at
instagram.com/swindali

# REFERENCES

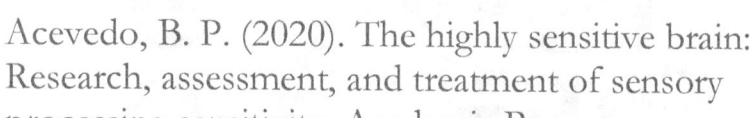

Acevedo, B. P. (2020). The highly sensitive brain: Research, assessment, and treatment of sensory processing sensitivity. Academic Press.

Clark, R.E. (2008). Building expertise: Cognitive methods for training and performance improvement. Wiley.

Cohen, E. (2024, May 3). Here's why you're feeling overstimulated — and what to do about it. Charlie Health. https://www.charliehealth.com/post/overstimulated

Cristol, H., Mitchell, K. & McPhillips, A. (n.d.). Dopamine: What it is & what it does. WebMD. https://www.webmd.com/mental-health/what-is-dopamine

Felton, A. (n.d.). Neurotransmitters: What to know. WebMD. https://www.webmd.com/brain/neurotransmitters-what-to-know

Forlini, E. (2023, May 19). Americans check their phones an alarming number of times per day. PC

Mag. https://www.pcmag.com/news/americans-check-their-phones-an-alarming-number-of-times-per-day

Henry Ford Health Staff (2023, December 1). How to identify and manage overstimulation. Henry Ford Health. https://www.henryford.com/blog/2023/12/how-to-identify-and-manage-overstimulation

Hu, E., Nguyen, A. (2022, April 4). Too much pleasure can lead to addiction. How to break the cycle and find balance. NPR. https://www.npr.org/2022/03/31/1090009509/addiction-how-to-break-the-cycle-and-find-balance

Lembke, A. (2021). Dopamine Nation: Finding balance in the age of indulgence. Penguin.

Mayo Clinic Health System. (2022, March 18). Cognitive overload: When processing information becomes a problem. https://www.mayoclinichealthsystem.org/hometown-health/speaking-of-health/cognitive-overload#:~:text=When%20there%20is%20too%20much,act%20on%20what%20is%20heard.

Medical News Today. (n.d.). What to know about sensory overload. https://www.google.com/url?q=https://www.medicalnewstoday.com/articles/sensory-overload%23faq&sa=D&source=docs&ust=1734068118776362&usg=AOvVaw2MLgVqHOYnEXOP5C5IkIfp

National Institute on Drug Abuse. (2024, August 13). Drugs and the brain. https://nida.nih.gov/publications/drugs-brains-behavior-science-addiction/drugs-brain

Rubinstein, J. S., Meyer, D. E., & Evans, J. E. (2001). Executive control of cognitive processes in task switching. Journal of Experimental Psychology: Human Perception & Performance, 27(4), 763–797. https://doi.org/10.1037/0096-1523.27.4.763

Samba Recovery. (2024, June 25). Average human attention span statistics & facts [2024]. https://www.sambarecovery.com/rehab-blog/average-human-attention-span-statistics

USC MAPP Online. (2023, November 17). Are there benefits of multitasking? USC Applied Psychology Blog. https://appliedpsychologydegree.usc.edu/blog/benefits-of-multitasking

Waters, J. (2021, August 22). Constant craving: How digital media turned us all into dopamine addicts. The Guardian. https://www.theguardian.com/global/2021/aug/

22/how-digital-media-turned-us-all-into-dopamine-addicts-and-what-we-can-do-to-break-the-cycle

Yale Medicine. How an addicted brain works. (2022, May 25). https://www.yalemedicine.org/news/how-an-addicted-brain-works

www.ingramcontent.com/pod-product-compliance
Lightning Source LLC
Chambersburg PA
CBHW071355160426
42811CB00094B/369